Dancing on the Ceiling:
Ceiling:
A Girl's Life and Beyond

Helene Maduff Rosenthal

iUniverse, Inc.
New York   Bloomington

Dancing on the Ceiling: A Girl's Life and Beyond

The views expressed in this work are solely those of the author and do not necessarily reflect the views of the publisher, and the publisher hereby disclaims any responsibility for them.

iUniverse books may be ordered through booksellers or by contacting:

iUniverse
1663 Liberty Drive
Bloomington, IN 47403
www.iuniverse.com
1-800-Authors (1-800-288-4677)

Because of the dynamic nature of the Internet, any Web addresses or links contained in this book may have changed since publication and may no longer be valid.

ISBN: 978-1-4502-2904-3 (sc)
ISBN: 978-1-4502-2905-0 (ebk)

Printed in the United States of America

iUniverse rev. date: 6/8/2010

This book is dedicated to
Our brave beautiful daughter Jennifer Rachel
And my wonderful mother
"Ever Lovin" Grandma Peggy

About the Cover

My daughter Jennifer's favorite flowers were yellow roses. Naomi's wedding bouquet was a combination of purple blossoms and yellow roses.

Lisa's bridal bouquet, on the cover of this book, contained a single yellow rose, surrounded by red ones. In this way, they each remembered and honored their sister, on their wedding days. This is just a single example showing that we continue to include Jenn in our lives.

Comments by People who Loved Jennifer

My wife has created a wonderfully loving tribute to our late daughter's life and her spirituality. I often think of our daughter Jennifer. She had a special gift which allowed her to inspire other people to do wonderful things. Since her death, people have honored her through their donations to charities, their providing books for children, creating programs to help cancer survivors, and raising funds for charities including but not limited to charitable walks, swims, and bike rides. This book further honors Jennifer.

I will always remember Jennifer's beautiful smile, her kind loving heart, special creativity, love for children, and spirituality. During the afternoon of the day she died, when she could no longer talk, I told her that she was my champion. A small tear appeared. Soon thereafter, she died. Jennifer, you will always be my champion!

Love, Dad

Bob Rosenthal

My older sister, Jennifer was diagnosed with leukemia when I was seventeen years old. At the time, I was too young and too naïve to know how to deal with my sister having a terminal illness. Nor did I realize what an impact her disease would have on my life, as well as the lives of my family.

As a teenager, my first action was to flee to a friend for comfort, but it didn't take long to realize that my life had taken a different path than my peers. They were lost in their dreams of school sports, high school plays and aspirations for their futures, while I was lost in the daze of uncertainty and anger, as to why this would happen to my twenty year old sister whose entire life seemed to be imprisoned by her disease.

I struggled with relationships and school, as I walked through the dark cloud my life had become, afraid of staying so close to someone who could be taken away. A strange reality set upon me in 1998 upon her passing, because I was just a few months younger than she was at the time of her diagnosis. It took years for the pieces of my life to fall back into place, and now at thirty one, I am wide eyed to the world around me as I realize that my sister's spirit has touched so many lives and changed them; especially the lives of my sister Lisa, parents Robert and Helene and myself.

I was the youngest family member and was often known as the comic relief (this title took me years to accept as my mother was convinced I would become a comedian}. I found my sister's passing to be the inspiration for my career of working as a Certified Veterinary Technician. Jennifer and I both loved animals, and had a menagerie of pets when we were growing up, which included:

rabbits, parakeets, hamsters, rats, and fish. We always found our animals comforting, especially our rabbits, and we constantly shared our dream of having our very own dog.

Ironically, I have done some work in Veterinary Oncology, where I assisted with the treatment of cats and dogs with different types of cancer. To me, the most important part of my job is being with the animals when they are near death or during euthanasia to make the last moments of their lives as calm and peaceful as possible. Many people ask me how I can watch the suffering of these sweet, innocent creatures, and I always tell them that I feel I am able to do it because of what I went through with my sister, Jennifer.

Naomi Paine

According to the Talmud, in each generation there are at least 36 righteous people on the planet, for who's sake the world is allowed to continue. The 36 are the "hidden ones", even to themselves. Still we can watch for them, treating each person as if they might be the one. By my third session with Jennifer, I felt privileged to think that I had finally met one of them, and I told her so. She was stunned, but then the 36 are said to be characterized by their humility. Jennifer was indeed humble, and was also deeply spiritual.

One day when I came to help her with her worsening illness, she told me she has a difficult problem. She wanted to insure that each of her friends received something of hers when she died. But she lamented, "I have more friends than I have possessions." We should all be burdened by such a problem!

Jennifer told me God had work for her to do--if not in this world, then in the next. As you will see in reading this delightful upbeat book, she began to work here, inspiring others while battling cancer and deepening her faith; and she continues to do even greater work from the other side.

It was such a gift to know her, and now you can meet her too!

Warren Nistad

Many "Thank Yous"

Our daughter, Jennifer, fought cancer for nearly two and a half years. During her battle, many friends, relatives, and other persons, showed how much they cared for her. Initially, she received blood and platelets from the community at large. After her dad, Bob, explained the importance of individual donors, many donors directed that their blood and platelets should be given to Jennifer. Even people who could not donate to Jenn because they lived out of our state, donated in their local communities. This out-pouring helped others who were in need. Her sister, Lisa, made another kind of donation, she took time off from her studies at the University of Arizona and went to Seattle to donate her bone marrow to Jenn.

I must give a special "thank you" to the Red Cross. Its chapters in Portland and Seattle provided critical support in obtaining, processing, and transporting blood and platelets so many times that I can't count, for Jennifer.

Many people visited Jennifer in both Portland and Seattle. In addition to her immediate family and Grandma Peggy from Portland, Grandma Shirley and Grandpa Ben came from Florida and Uncle Richard from New York. Her Aunt Debbie and Uncle Mike came from Colorado and Aunt Jackie from California. Her cousins arrived from Colorado, Maryland, California and Illinois. Her local and distant friends also visited with her. These visits, along with cards, gifts, and letters brightened her days. She especially appreciated notes and drawings from school children.

We met Jennifer's healer, Warren, in January of 1997. From that time on, he saw her almost every day. He visited her at home or in the hospital. These visits occurred frequently late at night, in order to help her sleep. Warren quickly became a friend to the entire family. He remains a friend and healer to our family today.

In the summer of 1997, two prayer services, for Jennifer, took place simultaneously in Portland. One was at Congregation Neveh Shalom and the other at Kesser Israel. Bob sent out an email notice so that people at other locations could pray for her at the same time.

Jenn's dad posted daily reports about her on the internet. Soon may people from around the world followed her story. Many of these people, even those who we didn't know, offered helpful suggestions.

As Lisa's college graduation approached, Bob asked for volunteers to watch over Jenn while Naomi, Bob, and I went to Arizona. Many people volunteered to stay with Jennifer. Her cousin Sheila came from Baltimore and her Aunt Jackie came from Los Angeles. They took turns at the hospital with Jenn. Her Uncle Bernie and others also took turns staying with her while we were gone.

My husband became very knowledgeable about leukemia. He conferred with Jennifer's doctors about medications and treatments. Jenn's sisters, Naomi and Lisa, were supportive and my mother, their Grandma Peggy visited Jenn often, and sometimes stayed with her to allow me some needed breaks. Jennifer also enjoyed visits with her fiancé, Brian and his family.

The religious communities in Portland and Seattle were also helpful. They often provided prayers and food for the family. Our rabbis also frequently came to our home, visited the hospital and mentioned Jennifer during religious services. I also wish to acknowledge the doctors and nurses who cared for Jenn. Even those taking and interpreting the hundreds of tests, showed great care and interest in her. The caring attitude extended all the way from lab courier to oncologist.

This story was inspired when I saw Jennifer's name spelled out along a highway on the road to Kona in Hawaii. This sign, as I explain in this book, let us know that she was there. After recalling this experience on paper, I realized that there was much more to share. Jenn inspired me to continue with her tale and guided me as I wrote.

Having Jennifer in my life for twenty two years was a joy and a challenge. For awhile, we had a wonderful family of five, a mom, dad, and three girls, but all too soon, there were only four of us. I will always miss our middle daughter, but I know that her spirit is with us.

I have not mentioned everyone who helped Jennifer and our family. All of her supporters are appreciated. Many of them continued to be there for us after she passed away.

Helene Rosenthal

Kewpie Doll

As we fly to Hawaiian skies,
My life flashes before my eyes.

My folks were happy when I was born,
Early on a November Morn.

One of the first photos of me,
Was taken in the hospital nursery.

They said that I was very small,
Mom said, "She looks like a Kewpie doll[1]."

They could not wait to share the news,
They had a second girl with baby blues.

When I went home, I met my big sis,
She gave me a little kiss.

Lisa liked to hold me in her lap,
When I got up from my nap.

In about three years, there came another,
A third daughter for my dad and mother.

A baby girl with eyes of brown,
Joined us in our Oregon town.

Because of my middle child jealousies,
Sometimes, I gave my baby sister's hand a squeeze.

Baby Jennifer

Top: Helene with Jennifer and Bob with Lisa
Lower: Jackie, Bernie, Debbie holding Danny, Mike,
Peggy, Sydney, Bob, Helene holding Jenn
Front: Shanah, Ari, and Lisa

Potty Chats

When we were little, we had lots of chats,
While on the potty, Naomi sat.

Later one of us, on the tub would sit,
And talk about this and that a bit.

We had these little chats for many years.
We shared our hopes and dreams and fears.

We talked about many things,
Including, how we liked to dance and sing.

We discussed the many friends we had,
And things to do with Mom and Dad.

We planned some funny musical skits
Sometimes we tumbled and did the splits.

There was another inspiration,
To tie string around our habitation.

Mom and Dad did not approve,
All the string we had to remove.

* * *

When Naomi was ten, I said her legs were scary,
Because they had gotten very hairy.

I used a razor but shaved too hard,
After that, her leg was scarred.

4

When it came in darker, she was not overjoyed,
Shaving often at a young age left her annoyed.

Family Trips

We all traveled a lot together,
To places with sunny or snowy weather.

We took driving trips both near and far,
The longest was from Portland to San Diego, in our car.

We went to Disney World and Disneyland.
Dad made sure our trips were thoroughly planned.

In Chicago, we visited many relations,
My favorite trips were Hawaiian vacations.

My first trek to Maui was in 1980,
When Naomi was still a little baby.

I loved going through the tunnel to Kaanapali,
Dad calls it "Jennifer's tunnel" because of me.

We stayed at a condo by the sea,
It was a very pleasant place to be.

Mom dressed us each in a Snoopy swimsuit,
She thought we all looked really cute.

Then she rubbed us with lotion so we would not burn,
She did our backs and then we'd turn.

We played in the sand by the ocean shore,
Laid in the sun and heard the waves roar.

We picnicked at a table by the ocean ,
And watched the sea's hypnotic motion.

We loved eating Hawaiian potato chips,
And taking cooling ocean dips.

Top: Grandma Shirley and Grandpa Ben with Lisa and
Jennifer
Lower: Helene holding Naomi, Bob and Jenn and Lisa in front

Many Activities

The three of us went to "Iddy Biddy Gymnastics".
Where we all learned lots of tricks.

We began by walking on the beam,
Like the big girls on the team.

We learned to roll and do the splits.
And we liked to jump into the pit.

As we got older, we worked on bars and floor.
We learned about aerials walkovers, leaps and more.

At seven, Lisa got on the gymnastic team,
To join her there was my dream.

I worked very hard to learn each routine,
We were often watched by our mom, Helene

I was five, when my gymnastic dream came true,
Our leos[2] were white and green and blue.

I was the littlest gymnast at my first meet.
I did not remember what to do with my hands and feet.

My coach helped me when I did floor,
By calling out moves I knew before.

As time went by, we did improve,
Then to another team, we had to move.

During this time, I also went to dance classes,
With lots of other little lasses.

When I was five, I had the chance,
At a county fair, to dance,

With friends at the Multnomah County Fair,
And a newspaper photographer was there.

For the "Oregon Journal" he took a photo for readers to
see,
Of a "Baleful Ballerina", Me!

I had a pink costume and dancing shoes,
Lisa also danced and wore a teeny tiny tutu too.

My sisters and I learned to swim,
And other miscellaneous activities were thrown in.

From school, to dance, to Hebrew lessons, I shifted
gears.
When I studied hard for several years,

To prepare for my Bat Mitzvah day,
While in Hebrew, I learned to sing and pray.

On the pulpit, I was scared and proud,
As I sang and prayed, before the crowd.

I stopped competing when I was thirteen,
Then spent more time on the dancing scene.

Remembering doing hand springs and flips,
Brings a smile to my lips.

Funny Bunny

I asked my mom and dad for a dog or cat,
They said "No." But later they let Naomi have a rat.

We had little blue parakeets,
Sometimes we fed them little birdie treats.

But I really wanted a soft and cuddly pet,
I said I would take care of it and not forget.

I thought "A bunny would be fun."
"I would play with her when my homework's done."

Mom took me to a store to find,
A little rabbit that would be mine.

We saw bunnies that were white and gray and brown
Some of their ears pointed up and others hung down.

I saw the sweetest little rabbit,
And said that I would really like to have it.

She was the color of caramel candy
And I named my new friend Taffy.

I really loved my little pet.
One day she got quite upset.

The T.V. was on a scary show,
We heard the volume grow and grow.

The music got so loud and shrill,
The bunny finally had her fill.

Taffy did not like the sound,
She jumped higher and higher off the ground.

She landed on Daddy's head and peed,
This was something he did not need.

The rest of us all laughed with glee,
'Cause this was such a funny sight to see.

Top: Jennifer at dance recital
Bottom: Jenn, Lisa, Ari, and Wendy in back
Shanah, Naomi, and Danny in front

Left: Jennifer's seashell search in Florida
Right: Autumn photo of Jenn

Top: Grandma Peggy and Jenn
Lower: Jennifer and Grandma Shirley

Top: Ari, Naomi, Shanah, Danny, Jennifer and Lisa
Bottom: Lisa, Naomi, Jennifer sitting and Wendy standing

Jenn, Lisa, and Naomi on Florida highway

Lots of Tots

I worked in day care for awhile,
Little ones always make me smile.

I took care of the smallest tots,
It was hard work, but I liked it lots.

A few years before, I took care of baby Manny,
Later, I wanted to be a nanny.

Luckily, I found a good position,
For a family with parents who were both physicians.

They had a baby boy named Ben,
I liked to play with him in the den.

I changed his diapers and washed his clothes,
When he slept, I peeked in to watch him doze.

Sometimes, early in the day,
We went to an indoor park to play.

Soon he had a little brother,
I was so happy to care for another.

Feeling Off

I was born in 1975,
For nineteen years, I grew and thrived.

For my twentieth birthday, I got a Pomeranian pup,
Ozzie's squeaky bark sometimes kept me up.

Soon I started feeling off,
I thought I was coming down with a cold or cough.

I brushed my teeth and flossed a lot,
But the hygienist said that I did not.

If the dentist had been there,
Perhaps he would have been aware,

That the signs should have been heeded,
A blood test was what I really needed.

Later, I burned my hand while I was cooking,
It soon got swollen and bad looking.

A red line went up my arm,
The doctor said the infection could do me harm.

But when the antibiotic did not do the trick,
He thought that I might be really sick.

Finally, blood from me was taken,
I was feeling very shaken.

Then the doctor said "Call your mom and dad."
That's when I knew it must be bad.

They met us in the examining room,
We all felt the doom and gloom.

On Mom's lap, I did sit,
We told the doctor to get on with it.

He let us know what was wrong,
It was time for us to all be strong.

This was the beginning of my fears,
About the leukemia I had for almost two and a half
years.

The doctors said I could wait one day,
Then I would start my hospital stay.

Mom went to my apartment to pack some clothing,
Get some other stuff together and then got going.

My roommates would take care of my little doggie,
They were very fond of Ozzie.

At my parents' house that night I stayed.
I cried a lot and then I prayed.

Cop Stop

In Arizona, Lisa heard the news and cried,
She got in her car for a quick short ride.

When she came to a rolling stop,
She was approached by a traffic cop.

He got out of his car and closed the door,
Went to her and asked what she was crying for.

Then she told him about me and said,
"I guess I will walk instead."

It was a short way to the sorority,
Where she could see her friends and talk about me.

Melissa thought she was crying about the traffic stop,
But Lisa told her that she was not.

She was feeling very bad,
This terrible news left her upset and sad.

Bess Kaiser Hospital

In the morning we took a ride,
Got to the hospital and went inside.

I settled into my hospital bed,
With a feeling of fear and dread.

The doctors did a lot of testing.
Then I did a lot of resting.

Things just went from bad to worse,
I thought that there must be a curse.

For we learned the leukemia was AML[3],
And it would be very hard for me to get well.

My boyfriend, Brian, I feared I would lose,
When he heard the awful news.

But he said he would not go away,
By my side he said he'd stay.

I was lying there worrying about my life,
When Brian asked me to be his wife.

I then said, "Yes, when my hair is long,
And once again, I'm feeling strong."

Then he gave me a beautiful ring,
Which made me want to dance and sing.

For awhile, I stopped my cryin',
Because, I was engaged to Brian.

Changing Floors

When I finished my first chemo round, I wanted to stop,
But Mom said she'd sleep over often on a cot.

Soon that hospital wouldn't be open anymore,
I was the last patient on the oncology floor.

As I held balloons, someone pushed my chair,
There was an eerie feeling in the air.

We headed from the south wing on the basement floor,
To a north side room on level four.

Mom, Dad and Brian escorted me,
Along with nurses and aides totaling three.

I could feel people who had passed before,
Following us on out the door.

Palm Springs

The doctors said I could go out of town,
Between my second and third chemo rounds.

So in March of 1996,
I went on one of my last trips.

To Palm Springs, four of us flew,
Me, Mom, Dad and Naomi, too.

We stayed at a Palm Desert time share resort,
I knew our time there would be too short.

I was so happy to swim in the pool,
Being in the water was really cool.

When I was outside after that,
I would wear a knit cap or a baseball hat.

We went to an outdoor museum,
There were lots of animals and I wanted to see 'em.

But it was too far for me to walk,
So Naomi and I had a talk.

I knew, on foot, I would be lagin',
So she agreed to pull me in a child size wagon.

The living desert had many gardens and a zoo,
There was a lot for us to see and do.

We saw zebras, warthogs, and gazelle,
Badgers, bobcats, and bighorn sheep as well.

Naomi trudged along for quite awhile,
She kept going for over a mile.

By the time we finished, Naomi was worn out,
She could hardly wait for me to get out.

The Living Desert and Wildlife and Animal Park,
Was so much fun, we stayed 'til it was almost dark.

Summer 1996

I felt better for awhile,
There were more times that I would smile.

Mom and I went shopping for new hair,
We shopped for a wig for me to wear.

We looked at straight and curly, short and long,
We saw black, red, brown, auburn, and blond.

After seeing all of those,
Long straight auburn is what I chose.

Putting it on was lots of fun,
I went outside and sat on a hydrant in the sun.

Then Mom took some pictures of me,
For many of our friends and relatives to see.

We went to a grocery store in the evening, where,
A lady said "You have such beautiful hair!"

"Thank you," was all I could think to say,
I didn't tell her, it was a wig I got that day

It looked nice but was uncomfortable on my head,
So, when I got home, I put it away and went to bed.

Naomi pulling Jennifer in wagon and Jenn wearing her wig

Relapse

After one round of chemo, I was in remission,
After two and three that was still my condition.

Then the doctor said, "You've relapsed Jenn,
It's time to think this through again".

"A bone marrow transplant could give you a chance,
To live your life and even dance."

We all went to get a blood test,
To see who would match me best.

Mom, Dad, Lisa, and Naomi had blood taken,
When I did it, I felt quite shaken.

I fainted because they took such a large amount,
They took more than I could count.

Mom was sitting on my right,
She got worried at the sight.

But she felt better when I got up soon,
And managed not again to swoon.

The human leukocyte antigen test was done,
To see if a family member would be the one,

To donate some marrow to me,
We all wondered who it would be.

Finally, we learned one day,
That I would go to Seattle for a three month stay.

Because Lisa's HLA[4] matched 6 of hers to 6 of mine,
We hoped, with help, I would soon be fine.

We discovered later, when I was in Washington state,
Even better that 6 to 6, Lisa and I matched 8 to 8.

Party Time

Many friends and relatives I did invite,
To a dinner party on a summer night,

So before going off to Washington,
I could see my friends and have some fun.

Brian, Michelle, and Nicole came,
My sisters, Grandma Peggy, and Mom and Dad did the
same.

Many others were also there,
To let me know how much they cared.

We were served lots of really good food,
For awhile, I was in a happy party mood.

Then it was time to say so long,
We all hoped I would come back well and strong.

Brian and Jennifer at dinner party.

Battle in Seattle

While in Seattle, I got a call,
From a man, I didn't know at all.

The synagogue we went to was the same,
He heard about me and got my number and name.

David was of my parents' generation,
And had a similar situation,

He thought a bone marrow transplant might be right for him,
And asked for me to clue him in.

The two of us talked many times more,
About our lives and what was in store.

* * *

Our apartment at First Hill was okay,
For the short time that I did stay.

Many clinic trips I made,
Before, at the hospital, I finally stayed.

There were many different patients there,
Many of them had no hair.

Lots of them were older than me,
And, also, there were little tots, whom I did see.

At the clinic I learned a lot.
About what to eat and drink and what I should not.

Also, that my immunities would go away,
I would need shots and inoculations again some day.

* * *

After I was settled in the hospital for awhile,
Lisa traveled many a mile.

She came to Seattle from the U of A,
It was a long journey for this special day.

Since all of my marrow was gone,
It was time for the transplant to be done.

After Lisa made this flying trip,
She had surgery to take marrow from her hip.

She was really quite a trooper,
Giving me her marrow was really super.

I stayed in my hospital room and waited,
Then came the moment we anticipated.

In a plastic bag was Lisa's marrow gift,
Maybe it would give my body a healthy lift.

In the afternoon at 15 to 3,
The infusion dripped into me.

Into my I.V. we watched it flow,
We prayed that it would make healthy new cells grow.

This was done on August twenty-sixth,
Of nineteen hundred and ninety-six.

We hoped the new marrow would thrive,
So I would have a chance to stay alive,

Lisa then went to the apartment with Mom,
Soon she started feeling warm.

She got dehydrated and very hot,
Fluids at the clinic helped a lot.

She flew back a bit too soon,
Returning to Phoenix in the afternoon.

Because her back was really sore,
She could not stay on the plane anymore.

To Tucson, a good friend drove her,
She was happy when the trip was over.

Mom slept over often, next to my bed,
Sometimes she talked and sometimes she read.

On weekday mornings, she turned on the T.V.,
To watch "Live with Regis and Kathie Lee."

Later in the mornings on the telly.
She watched "Live with Regis and Kelly."

I wished my dreams of health would come true,
When finally Lisa's marrow grew.

My new marrow did appear,
In the middle of September of that year.

If I got well, I had a great desire,
To sing along, in the synagogue choir.

Visitors from Near and Far

Most weekends by car, my dad did travel,
To visit Mom and me in Seattle.

My sister, Naomi, would tag along,
And often she was heard singing an old camp song.

Luckily, there wasn't too much rain.
Sometimes, Grandma Peggy came in by train.

Grandma Shirley and Grandpa Ben came to visit me,
And Uncle Richard, I also did see.

Other friends and relatives came, over my three month
stay,
Many traveled from far away.

Food was brought to us by people in two congregations,
They liked to help people in difficult situations.

For the High Holidays, at the hospital, I had to remain,
So, from a local synagogue, two people came.

For Rosh HaShanah, we had a short service one day.
So I could pray with others for the holiday.

Mom, Dad, and I followed along,
As we read with them and joined in song.

* * *

As I got better, the nurses told me to exercise,
I thought, what they said was very wise.

So I walked around the bone marrow transplant floor,
Then turned around and walked some more.

Later, I walked in downtown Seattle,
Going up the hills was quite a battle.

To the Space Needle Brian and I went,
For a short time, I felt content.

My folks and I went to some stores and out to eat,
Going to restaurants again was quite a treat.

Since my immune system was impaired,
With caution, from more difficulties, I could be spared.

Sometimes, we asked questions, so we could be sure,
That the food I ate was safe and pure,

For after a transplant, it is best to know the food's okay,
So it won't create problems in any way.

*Top: Grandpa Ben, Grandma Shirley, Uncle Richard, and
Lisa in Seattle hotel
Lower: Jenn, Dan, Naomi, Shanah and Lisa*

Home Again

In November, Mom drove me to our home state.
Getting back to Portland was really great.

On my 21st birthday, a few friends, came over for
awhile,
Their birthday visit made me smile.

But soon that smile was wiped away,
When I heard what my doctor had to say.

Mom was with me when he phoned, renewing my fears,
When I got the news, my eyes filled with tears.

I had to fight the disease once more,
I knew a lot of bad days were in store.

I went to a healer on Northwest 23rd,
Until from my rabbi I got the word,

There was a member of our congregation,
Who had another recommendation,

To the hospital or her home, her healer came,
To help her heal and lessen pain.

He'd kept her going for a long time more,
Than the doctors said, some years before.

It was truly her belief,
That he could give me some relief.

Mom arranged for Warren to meet me.
I heard his chuckles before he could greet me.

As he came to my bedroom from the hall,
I could see that he was fairly tall.

He had a full head of golden hair,
I knew that he would really care.

Since he was always full of cheer,
My dad called Warren, the "Happy Healer".

My sister Lisa took a different stand,
She often called him the "Voodoo Man"

The next time he came, he photographed me,
My short hair and smile, he liked to see.

Since the hair was off my shoulders and face,
And of make up, there was no trace,

My friend, Aviva liked this picture of me,
Because, my spirit, shining through, she could easily see.

"Beaches" was a movie that Aviva and I adored,
I could watch it many times and not be bored.

We also liked when Bette Midler sings,
Especially the song, "The Wind Beneath my Wings".

We debated and neither of us would give in,
We each thought the other one of us was the wind.

When I was twenty one, I had the chance to see
Bette Midler sing and dance, as if for me.

Our seats were up high. It was hard to see,
But I was pleased Dad got tickets for him, Naomi, Mom
and me.

I could not drink, but I was twenty-one,
And I thought to buy one would be fun,

So I got some wine for my dad.
Seeing me happy made him glad.

The three of us had a great night,
The "Devine" Bette was a real delight.

* * *

One day at my home, when Warren came in,
He had a chuckle and a great big grin.

In his hand was the framed photo of a rose.
It was a special picture that he chose.

Many pictures of roses he had taken,
But there was no mistakin',

The Peace Rose is a beautiful variety,
He said its beauty reminded him of me.

It has a touch of pink on its yellow bloom,
And it gives off a sweet perfume.

For yellow roses, I developed a great affection,
Mom now has a yellow rose collection.

She also realized that by our driveway,
There was a Peace Rose bush on display.

Warren's photo of Jennifer and Jenn with Warren

Las Vegas

After more chemo, at the hospital on Sunnyside,
I felt good enough to go for a plane ride.

So early in '97, once again in remission,
I went to Las Vegas, with my doctor's permission.

Since I had turned twenty one,
We decided to go there and have some fun.

Mom, Brian, Dad and I traveled by plane,
Happy to be away from the Oregon rain.

We stayed at Ceasar's Palace,
Where we met Lisa, my big sis.

From Tucson, with some friends she came,
To visit with us and play some games.

In a borrowed wheelchair, I was pushed around,
Las Vegas' streets, in the Nevada town.

It was really good, going out in the sun,
Seeing the sights, was lots of fun.

There were water shows and a pirate ship,
Palm trees, flowers, and cactus along the strip.

At the Mirage, Mom and I bought some logo T's,
And a sweatshirt with several colorful palm trees.

We saw white tigers, crouched behind glass,
They ignored us, when we went past.

We went to an "all you can eat" buffet,
There was plenty of food on every tray.

The others all had a lot to eat,
I just nibbled my meal and had something sweet.

When it was almost time to fly away,
Mom took pictures of Brian and me at the "Hard Rock
Café".

Spring 1997

My friend, David, decided to change his provider,
Went ahead and switched to Kaiser.

After he made that change,
At Sunnyside Hospital, a meeting was arranged.

Often in room 116, I would stay,
The number is Lisa's January birthday, month and day.

David's hospital room was across the hall from mine.
We saw each other several times.

His wife and little girl, I met too,
Sometimes, they visited me in my hospital room.

To Sunnyside Hospital, Warren asked a lady to come to see me.
She was the mother of a friend of Naomi.

A woman, named Kathy, who could see angels, visited before too long.
She said she felt my spiritual personality which was very strong.

It was January 26th, 1997,
She had come to look for spirits from heaven.

At our meeting, she was so pleasantly surprised,
That she was overcome and cried.

When asked if angels were present as well,
A poster moved off the wall and fell.

She saw an angel watching over me with care,
And many of my ancestors surrounded me there.

With my grandma, there was another,
Grandma Peggy thought it was her mother.

Kathy drew two pictures to show us where they were,
Several with me and one with her.

I drew a picture too, for my dad,
To remind him of all the fun we had.

When I was little, we drew pictures together.
So I drew him a house and playground in sunny
weather.

Fevers and Hallucinations

That spring, after three chemo rounds,
There were very few smiles and many frowns.

I was to leave the hospital with my mom and dad,
But then things got to be very bad.

My temperature started to rise,
My body also increased in size.

I got a fever and started to shiver,
And there were worries about my liver.

To lower the fever, ice packs were put around,
They helped to bring my fever down.

And although my hands were swelling,
Mom was able to remove one ring.

The other one would not slide,
No matter how hard she tried.

It became clear
On March 27th of the year,

It was necessary to remove the second one.
That was easier said than done.

So someone came to cut the band,
Just to get it off my hand.

This did not go very well,
It hurt so much, it made me yell.

Down the hall, Dad heard me scream,
Too bad this wasn't just a dream.

There was some bleeding and relief,
That finger no longer gave me grief.

* * *

Sometimes Mom wanted to give me a hug or pat,
But I said no to all of that.

I did not want to feel her touch,
Because it just hurt too much.

I was given morphine to ease the pain,
It did funny things to my brain.

I was on so many medications,
That I had strange dreams and hallucinations.

One time, I thought a dog was on my bed,
But it was Brian's hairy arm instead.

Then there were clowns everywhere,
But they no longer scared me, I didn't care.

Another time, a jockey outfit, I had on,
While on a brown horse, I raced along.

A nurse watched the race and bet on me.
Also, in my dreams, lots of parties, I could see.

They mostly occurred at night,
Costumed people were quite a sight.

There was a lot of dancing there,
And on a ship, I had fancy dresses to wear.

There was a hotel made out of candy where I stayed.
And on a boat in a storm, Warren and I prayed.

Intensive Care

That spring was among the worst,
For a week, we didn't know my appendix burst.

Although, with surgery, it came out okay,
There was an infection that probably wouldn't go away.

I didn't know my appendix was gone,
I could not remember what went on.

At the time, I was in remission,
But even if there was a change in my condition,

I could not do chemo again,
Because the infection would surely win.

Part of the time, in the ICU,
I had a male nurse, who knew just what to do.

He was a former military man who was very strict,
A better nurse could not be picked.

He worked hard and long through the first night,
To Mom and Dad it was a scary sight.

My blood pressure went down to 35,
But somehow he managed to keep me alive.

When Warren came, my vital signs still were not good,
So then he did what he could.

And after only a few minutes with me,
Everyone was surprised to see,

That the readings, once again were all right,
Things had improved, according to every blinking light.

Because of these two men, I grew stronger,
So I was able to live longer.

It would have been quite nice,
If I could have had something other than ice.

But my stomach had to make a gurgling sound,
So that my food and drink would stay down.

I spent many days in intensive care,
Wishing I could get out of there.

The Storm

Very early on an April morning,
While outside, it was storming,

Warren came in while I was sleeping.
Then I awoke, with a start, from dreaming.

I opened my eyes in a darkened room,
Where I saw him in the gloom.

When he arrived that night,
I said, "Is everything all right?"

He replied, "The power's down,
And the wind is pushing trees almost to the ground."

I had awoken from my snooze,
With a bad case of the blues.

I was very fearful and depressed,
I felt unhappy and very stressed.

Warren said, "To stop feeling that way,
It is time to meditate and pray."

He said that ruach[5] was out there,
The breath of life and spirit in the air.

"The ruach has come to heal you.
So use the wind that's passing through."

An I.C.U. nurse had her schedule changed,
To be with us that night, she arranged.

For she knew that soon, I might leave,
But in miracles, she wanted to believe.

So she stayed with Warren and me,
Hoping there would be one for her to see.

Warren and the nurse worked together,
While outside, there was windy, stormy weather.

I said that my stomach was very sore,
And wished it would not hurt anymore.

The nurse had an idea, which she did explain,
To use guided imagery to ease the pain.

She said, "Think of Hawaii when it's really hot,
Picture yourself, lying on a beach, in a sunny spot."

She told me, "Just use your hand,
To put on your stomach some very hot sand."

"That hot and heavy sandy dirt,
Will take away the pain and hurt."

My tummy felt good when I was done,
Imagining lying on the beach in the sun.

I felt better than I had before,
And knew that I would be around many days more.

A brighter day had finally come,
For I was still there to see the sun.

The nurse felt a miracle had occurred that night,
I was still alive to see the morning light.

For two weeks I was in the ICU,
Until the oncology floor would do.

The oncology nurses thought I would not last much
more,
That I would not go back to the oncology floor.

So the nurses were surprised to learn,
That to their floor, I would soon return.

They did not know why,
It was not my time to die.

The morning after the storm went away,
I went back to a regular room for the rest of my stay.

* * *

My parents wanted to go to Arizona soon,
To see Lisa graduate in the afternoon.

From Tuscon's U of A,
For several days they would be away.

Dad sent out an email plea,
To ask friends or relatives to stay with me.

Mom's cousin Sheila said she'd come,
And my Aunt Jackie was another one.

The two of them came from far away,
To Oregon from Baltimore and L.A.

They took turns and some others did too,
Keeping me company in my hospital room.

My Uncle Bernie stopped by too,
We talked about pictures that I drew.

* * *

In the hospital I usually had a three week stay,
But that spring it did not turn out that way.

At Sunnyside Hospital, I met a lady with AML.
She was someone who Warren helped as well.

I said," I just broke the record with my hospital stay,
I've been here for a total of 65 days."

Carol replied, "That makes me sad.
When we leave here, I will be glad."

I went home after my tenth week,
In my own bed, it was good to sleep.

As Warren helped me out one night,
There was a very surprising sight,

I saw Carol with us too that day,
Two days before, she had passed away.

* * *

One day I was relaxing, while I watched T.V.
When Mom set up my I.V.

I was getting my hydration,
When I got a strange sensation.

It felt like a bubble was in my chest,
We called the nurse, who said, "Just rest."

"It will be okay,
In a little while, it will go away."

Mom said, "No one flushed the line,
On other days, it was always fine."

After that, she made sure it was just right,
So I would not have another fright.

* * *

David and others with AML, wanted a special name,
To make us feel strong, in spite of fear and pain.

To live as long as we could, we kept on trying,
We thought of the name Amazing Miraculous Lions.

David and I kept in touch by phone.
He got me a box with special stones.

Shortly after this world he left,
His wife brought me that special gift.

"Send in the Clowns" played when I opened the box.
It was filled with what he called "me sheberocks[6]".

He sent a message, that I should carry on,
I should be strong, even though he was gone.

I barely knew him, for a very short time,
But David was a special friend of mine.

* * *

Only a short time did elapse,
When once again, I did relapse.

We took one more short family trip,
Before I got to be too sick.

To Skamania Lodge, Dad drove, Mom, my sisters and me,
So we could have special time as a family.

We had dinner there that night,
Outside the view was quite a sight.

There were many trees and grass so green
It was quite a pretty scene.

Later a hanger was placed above my bed,
To set up an I.V. above my head.

After breakfast we walked around,
Along the paths on the hotel grounds.

Lots of pictures were taken of us all,
Some of us sitting on rocks and some standing tall.

Top: Lisa, Naomi, Jenn, and Bob at Skamania Lodge
Middle: Jenn and Grandpa Ben

Worn Out

Early in '98, when the infection had not done me in,
Mom said, "Jenn, please go get tested again."

Finally, to do this I did agree,
The doctors were amazed, because, no infection could they see.

Mom thought that I could do more chemo,
But she did not know,

That I was just too worn out,
And the doctors did not have a doubt,

That it was too late for me,
To receive anymore chemotherapy.

They knew, I could not survive much longer,
It might have worked if I was stronger.

Mom got upset and started to cry,
Because she did not want to say, "Good-by."

I called her friend, Barbara, in San Diego,
So she would let my mother know,

That she could always talk to Barb,
Especially when the days are very hard.

Taking medication was too much of a chore,
And I didn't want blood drawn anymore.

I asked my parents to let me stay at home,
So I would not be alone.

I wanted my special things near me,
And I needed to be with friends and family.

I promised Mom that I would wait,
'Til after she had her birthday cake.

Then I would not take pills anymore,
I knew many bad days were in store.

But, I would still continue to pray.
That a miracle would come to me one day.

Home Movie

We heard about a movie, in 1998,
That people said was really great.

I could not go to see it shown,
So it was delivered to my home.

A man flew to Portland, from faraway,
He brought us a special film from L.A.

In the living room, we all gathered,
Watching the movie was all that mattered.

I watched it with my sisters, my dad, Bob and my mom,
Helene.
It was the best movie, I'd ever seen.

Its name is a secret, I cannot tell,
Although, a big "Thank You", I want to yell.

More Visitors

I spent many days in my bed,
With gloomy thoughts in my head.

It felt better when I saw things outside my room,
Like people and animals and flowers in bloom.

When I looked out, I could see the trees,
And the wind blowing through the leaves.

Sometimes, I heard the breeze softly sigh,
At other times, it came roaring by.

My friend Aviva came from far away,
To talk with me and help me pray.

She took care of me one night,
So Mom could sleep 'til it was light.

My cousin, Shanah, stayed with me, one night too,
To help me and keep me company in my room.

Dad's friend Alice, and some others, came to perform
for me,
Some songs and dances from Hawaii.

A Hawaiian banner they did hang,
And about a hukilau they sang.

A guitar and ukulele were both played.
I watched from a chair, where I stayed.

My mom and dad even took a chance,
And tried to do a hula dance.

In the past, I would have joined the fun,
But at the time, it could not be done.

I enjoyed the visit and the show,
But it made me long to go,

To my favorite places in Hawaii once more,
And to play in the sun on the Maui shore.

* * *

A friend told a lady musician ,
About my serious medical condition.

Maureen said if I would agree,
She'd come to play her harp for me.

To our home, she brought her instrument,
Maureen and her harp were heaven sent.

Beautiful music tickled my ears,
And to my eyes brought happy tears.

It was a very wonderful way,
To bring joy to me on that special day.

* * *

Mom had asked Dad to make arrangements for when I
was gone,
This was something that she would not take on.

She knew of a girl we had seen on T.V.
Who passed away a long time before me.

She was a member of our congregation,
Where I went for some of my early education.

When she was around my age, her life was taken,
Many, many hearts were broken.

Mom thought it would be good for me,
If near her, my resting place would be.

So that when my earthly life did end,
I could right away, make a new friend.

Dad checked many places and picked out a spot,
Not knowing what my mother thought.

Mom was very surprised to find,
That Rebecca's spot was next to mine

Over there, a special rose bush grows,
It blooms with my favorite flower, the yellow Peace
Rose.

From there, on special days, balloons are now sent to me,
It's a very pretty sight to see.

Balloons are yellow, green, blue, and pink,
With messages written in indelible ink,

Telling how Mom and Dad miss me and send their love,
Then they watch as the balloons float and disappear above.

Some for Rebecca are also let go,
They quickly rise up from below.

Harpist Maureen Love and Jennifer

Goodbye and Hi

A nurse came to help me near the end.
She became a special friend.

Then Naomi came to say "Good by."
And seeing me made her cry.

Though, I was unconscious, I still heard,
Her every single spoken word.

I heard this last chat.
She talked while on my bed she sat.

She held my hand in hers,
As she said those final words.

I felt an electric shock go through me,
From my hand into Naomi.

That was the time I really passed,
But it was not when I breathed last.

Though I was free, I lingered on,
Until it was almost dawn.

Many psalms, the nurse read to me that night,
She read 'til it was almost light.

All around me, everything was very bright,
And I felt so wonderfully light.

There would be no more transfusion, no more pain,
No more morphine or chemo fogging up my brain

For awhile, I drifted in the dark,
Then in the distance, I saw a spark,

That spark turned into a light,
A fabulous, glowing, dazzling white.

Then in the distance, I could see,
Friends and relatives waiting for me.

There were people there, I did not know,
Because they passed away, long ago,

Many men and children and ladies,
And lots of my family's bubbies and zadies[7]

I hugged Grandpa Sydney and Uncle Ty,
I was so happy, I could almost cry.

And other relatives, I never knew,
Were all there, waiting to greet me too.

Early in the morning, my family knew I'd gone,
Now, without me they had to carry on.

* * *

A day after I passed away, Dad had flowers sent,
To my friend, Warren, from me, as a special present.

It was a yellow rose bouquet,
To thank him after I went away.

When he got them, he was so surprised,
For a long time after, he cried and cried.

Dancing on the Ceiling

I passed away at twenty-two years,
Friends and relatives shed many tears.

Even people who did not know me, cried,
When they heard that I had died.

Some time later, I heard Warren say:
"Please come to me, Jennifer, right away."

In just a moment, I was there,
Floating high up in the air.

When I arrived, I was so elated,
That to myself, I stated:

"Oh, how happy I am feeling,
Up here dancing on the ceiling."

I then saw, a lady on a bed,
With healing hands upon her head.

Then I looked and saw our healer,
That is when I clearly heard her.

"There's a pretty girl dancing on the ceiling,
With long brown hair that she's revealing."

Even though he knew it was true,
Warren wished that he could see me too.

I remember when I was the one,
Who could not sing or dance or run.

Now that I am strong again,
I'm feeling like a healthy Jenn.

* * *

Warren told Mom, there would be
Many more events amazing,

People would get signs from me
That would send hearts racing.

One day I went to my parents' home,
I was there all alone.

Naomi's friend and little boy passed by,
I saw them and I waved "Hi."

Even though, he hadn't known me,
He said he saw the sister of Naomi.

His mom was so startled by what he'd said,
She took his hand and then they fled.

Aloha

One day, shortly, before I passed,
Mom sat down on my bed and asked,

"When the rest of us go to Hawaii as planned,
Would you please write your name in the sand?"

I said that I would surely try,
So you will know that I'm nearby.

I joined my family on this healing trip,
We traveled at a steady clip.

To Hawaii, they had come,
To relax and enjoy the tropical sun.

They rounded up all of their suitcases,
So they could move on to other places.

They came to Kona for a one week stay,
To grieve, to rest, to tour, and play.

In Hawaii, I too, did arrive,
Knowing in a way, I'm still alive.

The Hawaiian sky was a beautiful blue,
With fluffy white clouds passing through.

There was the tang of ocean breeze,
And salty air drifting over from the seas.

But they barely noticed the island air,
Through their heart ache and despair.

Going to Kona was their plan,
So Dad drove them in a rented van.

In the car, they all were brooding,
While thoughts of me kept intruding.

Some flowers bloomed along the way,
Brightening up a very sad day.

There was graffiti flying by,
White coral and black lava caught the eye

There were some hearts and many names,
Like Lani, Michael, Jack, and James.

There's the sign I made appear,
By whispering into someone's ear.

It came out differently than I planned.
It wasn't written in the sand.

On black lava, foot high white letters spell,
My name "Jennifer" which they know so well.

Mom thought, "I must turn my head,
In case Jenn's name is here, like she said."

She then looked around to find,
My great big newly written sign.

Then she asked the others, "Did you notice?
Jennifer left a message for us."

Mom was smiling as she cried,
Tears were dripping from her eyes.

The others did not see it then,
But they knew, they would come again.

They came back very soon,
To take pictures in the afternoon.

* * *

After the drive from the Kona Airport,
We all arrived at the Kona Coast Resort.

They all liked this heavenly location,
It was ideal for a peaceful vacation.

From the balcony, could be seen,
People golfing on the green.

They could go to the pool for a swim,
And Dad would spend some time in the gym.

Jennifer's sign on Queen Kaahumanu Highway
On the ocean side between Old Kona Airport and Kona

We stopped at a restaurant for lunch,
The waitress there had a hunch,

"Do you need a table for five? she asked.
(That's what it was in the past.)

Though Mom said it was just for four,
They really knew it was for one more.

The fifth seat looked empty, but it was not,
For I was sitting in that spot.

Mom took a picture of an empty chair,
But they all knew that I was there.

* * *

They took some drives along the Pacific shore,
And found some time to explore.

Sometimes they would forget me for awhile,
And then they would even laugh and smile.

One morning they all got up early,
Naomi was very groggy and sleepy.

For about an hour they rode in the car.
And all this time, I never went far.

Then they stopped for a chopper ride.
Dad and Lisa climbed inside.

Naomi and Mom, then drove to some stores,

While in the car, Mom heard her snores.

When Naomi finally finished her rest,
They went to the Waikaloa resort that was one of the best.

There were boats and trains to ride,
While people watched the ocean tide.

By the Kona Pool they ate,
And left before it got too late.

Next they picked up Lisa and Dad.
And told them about the fun they had.

Then they went back there right away,
To see the dolphins swim and play.

Later, the girls rented bikes and coasted down,
From the resort, for a few miles into town.

I saw my sisters, Lisa and Naomi,
As they rode there bikes below me.

They stopped when they reached the rocky shore,
Relaxed awhile and rode some more.

Traveling Abroad with Lisa

The land of Israel, I always wanted to see,
But never had the opportunity.

Lisa sold my car and used money I left her in my will,
So through her, my wish I could fulfill.

Soon after the Hawaii trip, she traveled again,
To Israel and other places, far from Oregon.

With a single backpack she went to a different part of the
world,
A great adventure, for her, unfurled.

At the beginning of her exciting trip.
She had her first stop in Cairo, Egypt.

While there, she had a private tour,
With a guide and driver just for her.

Lisa visited a pyramid and other sites,
She stayed in Egypt for about five nights.

Then to Israel, my big sister flew,
She saw Jerusalem, old and new.

In the new city, with friends she stayed,
And went to the "Western Wall[8]" where many people
prayed.

When Lisa was at the "Wailing Wall",
She thought about me most of all.

The Dead Sea was really grand,
But Lisa's watch was taken or lost in the sand.

From there she went climbing up to Masada[9].
And later visited cousins in Be'er Sheva[10]

After two weeks in Israel she said "Farewell".
From Tel Aviv, she left Eretz, Yisrael[11]

Over the Mediterranean , she flew,
To Athens in Greece, where there was lots to see and do.

From there to the Acropolis, she took a train,
Shortly after she arrived, her soul was filled with pain.

Looking up at the Acropolis, she fell apart,
She grieved and cried for me, with an aching heart.

Then Lisa pulled herself together once more
And then continued to expore.

Ferry rides took her to two Greek isles,
At one of them she rode in style,

On a moped, along with some American and Australian guys,
And stopped at cliffs with views of water and blue skies.

Some of the fellows jumped and she said she would too.
They thought it was an unwise thing for her to do.

When she jumped, they were surprised by this unexpected event,
And were amazed when she somersaulted for her second descent.

Next, it was on to Italy, the first stop was Rome.
She liked it so much, she felt right a home.

She traveled to Florence, Pisa, Venice, Verona and Milan.
Soon after that, she had fun in Switzerland,

While canyoning[12] in Interlaken, she got soaked,
From a waterfall and rappelling on a rope.

And in a river, she went slipping and sliding down,
It looked like so much fun, I'm glad I was around.

Once again she settled in a railroad car,
From Interlaken to Paris was not too far,

In Paris, France she spent many a happy hour,
At museums, parks, and the Eifel Tower.

At Orly Airport she got on a plane,
And journeyed many hours 'til she was home again.

During this trip, I was close at hand,
Enjoying with Lisa, all of those foreign lands.

Naomi and Warren

That summer, Naomi's back was hurting,
She arranged for Warren to do some healing.

After a massage that was long and soothing,
Naomi felt herself relaxing.

Then Warren's hands hovered in the air,
Above Naomi's hand and hair.

The next thing that they knew,
Her hand was up there too.

It wasn't what they had expected,
When it moved like they were connected.

Naomi was like a puppet on a string,
Warren thought it was the funniest thing.

He thought this was a funny jest,
But finally stopped to let her arm rest.

Another Jennifer

Shortly after I passed away,
My folks talked to a reporter one day.

They told about happy times in my life,
And about the many days of strife.

They talked about another Jennifer, too,
An 18 year old girl I slightly knew.

She was a few years younger than me.
Since our dads worked together, I knew her and her
family.

Early in 1996, she was inspired by my situation,
And told other students about bone marrow donations.

She talked to many high school teens,
About, what being a born marrow donor means.

At a blood drive, a little extra blood they would be
giving,
To be typed for a bone marrow donor listing.

Getting donors was not an easy task,
Twenty four students did what she asked.

And even better, in 1998,
The number rose to one hundred and eight.

Much money would be needed,
And by some groups, the call was heeded.

Exactly, one month after I passed,
"Jennifers' Stories" appeared in the Oregonian at last.

The Collin's Medical Trust gave a $26,000 grant, donation,
To help with a handbook, website, and video information.

In 1999, awards were given to heroes in Oregon,
One of them was Jennifer Opton.

On March tenth, the "Breakfast of Champions" took place.
She received a "Wheaties" box with a picture of her face.

* * *

In 1998, my parents learned in October,
That the doctors I worked for, donated to a shelter.

A beautiful bookcase made of oak,
With an inscription that said:
"WHERE THERE IS LIFE, THERE IS HOPE."[13]

It was filled with books, dedicated with my name,
For the children, who to this shelter came.

The Domestic Violence Resource Center is a place,
Where moms and children can be safe.

At the Oregon Shore

Naomi and some friends took the highway,
Not knowing that they were "going my way".

It was a long car ride,
To go and watch the Oregon tide.

To Rockaway beach they did go,
To play on the sand and watch a bonfire glow.

Naomi and a friend hiked along the beach on a lark,
The early morning was chilly and dark.

The two girls walked on the sand.
And Naomi was feeling grand.

When they were on the Oregon shore,
Naomi felt so good, she twirled and twirled some more.

Both of them were suddenly aware,
That there was a change in the air.

I wrapped around my sister with a nice warm breeze,
As she fell down laughing on her knees.

Then she heard me laughing too.
That I was there, Naomi knew.

Sunriver

For her eightieth birthday, Grandma Peggy and Ari flew to Sunriver,
For a party and presents that others would give her.

Lisa was the one who got everyone together,
In the snowy, cold, and stormy weather.

Uncle Mike and Aunt Debbie came with Danny and Shanah,
And my sisters were there with Daddy and Mama.

Brian stopped by the first night with Nathan, his friend,
And visited my family, at the rented house near Bend.

I joined Naomi and Shanah for a schmooze,
And Shanah shared some exciting news.

She was quite pleased to say,
She'd found a guy she liked in every way.

Because of the boyfriend her cousin had,
Naomi was feeling very glad.

They both felt that I was there,
And, believed I too, did care.

Somehow, they knew,
That for Shanah, I was happy too.

The next day, at Mt. Bachelor, Naomi went skiing with
Lisa and Danny.
While Naomi was there, she fell on her fanny,

She looked so funny with her skis in the air,
That Dan took a picture of her sitting there.

When he was done, he gave her a hand,
Pulled her up and helped her stand.

Eleven people got together that night to dine,
Grandma's eightieth birthday was a happy time.

Blood Drive

In Portland, the Fred Meyer Corporation,
Asked employees for a blood donation.

Brian's mom, in a memo, made a plea,
To have others help people like me.

Laurel said I was important to her and times had been
rough.
"Platelets and a bone marrow transplant were not enough."

At the blood drive, done in my honor,
Everyone was asked to be a potential bone marrow
donor.

The response was really great,
For many pints, people did donate.

The total pints donated was 152,
Over the goal of 130 by 22.

This was in the fall of the year before 1999,
Mom thought some of the numbers were a sign,

Because the number 22 was on the page,
And I passed away at that same age.

And the 113 bone marrow typings, looked at in a certain
way,
Include my birthday number, 11 for the month, and 13
for the day.

A Good Dream

On the night before two years after my leaving,
My mom was in her bed dreaming.

I came to her, as I was, when I was two,
To let her know, I was as good as new.

She picked me up and gave a hug,
Both of us could feel the love.

She felt my body, soft and warm,
And I could feel myself in her arms.

Mom knew that this was real,
Because, my weight, she could truly feel.

That morning, with happy thoughts, she awoke,
Knowing, with my absence, she would better cope.

Long Walks

In the spring of 2000, Mom took many long strolls,
Practicing for "Suzuki, Rock and Roll".

 She joined Portland's team TNT[14],
To raise money for people like me.

While she walked, she made up rhymes,
And picked up quarters, pennies, nickels, and dimes.

Sometimes, I heard her singing softly,
A song she made up just for me:

"Oh Jennifer, my Jennifer, I miss your dancing feet.
Oh Jennifer, my Jennifer, I miss your voice so sweet".

"I miss your smiles, I miss your frowns,
I miss your ups, I miss your downs,"

"I even miss your fear of clowns,
My love for you abounds".

"The rest of us must carry on,
Now that you are really gone."

"But there is something you should know,
Our love for you will always grow."

In case she tried to walk 26.2,
A 20 mile practice walk she had to do.

"I'll continue, if Jenn gives me a 26 cent sign."
She thought, "then I'll do it just one time."

On the next day, she found,
A quarter and a penny I left on the ground.

She did complete the 20 mile trip one day,
And took the long walk on the thirteenth of May.

In San Diego, she walked halfway,
In a 26 mile marathon, on a very hot day.

A stomach ache slowed her down for awhile,
But just in time, she completed her thirteenth mile.

Mom finished without mishap, but Dad was in pain,
While he waited, he tripped and got an ankle sprain.

Shanah's Wedding

Cousin Shanah wanted me to come to her wedding
celebration,
But did not known how to give me an invitation.

Mom said, "All you have to do is tell her.
But, I can go ahead and ask her healer."

Mom knew, he'd reached me before,
And was sure that he could do it once more.

When Warren finally contacted me,
For fun, I said, "I'll come if I like the colors. What will
they be?"

Mom, Dad, Lisa, and Naomi went a long way,
To be in Denver on Shanah and Josh's wedding day.

At the dinner, Mom was a little out of kilter,
As if sights and sounds came through a filter.

She felt peculiar because I was there,
Sometimes right by her in her chair.

My Friend Laura

My Dad was on the board of a charitable organization,
Cancer Care was its designation.

People there gave support and information,
To help cancer patients and their families in a difficult
situation.

My friend Laura had a big surprise,
When she asked to help cancer patients exercise.

When she learned the funding was in honor of me, her
friend who died,
She was so overcome that she cried.

Warren's Birthday Party

At Warren's birthday party in 2005,
His friend Laura O. saw me arrive.

Behind Naomi, I stayed for awhile,
Laura saw my curly hair and happy smile.

At the same time, my sister felt me there,
She shivered as I stood behind her chair.

For only a short time, Laura saw me,
When I had my encounter with Naomi.

Everyone is pleased to know,
That to Warren's party, I did go.

Chanukah Time

Four years later, on December 12th, 2009,
I stopped at my parent's house at Chanukah time.

My mom, dad, sisters, their families and some friends,
All were pleased and happy to attend.

There were latkes[15] and many other good things to eat,
And some delicious peanut butter chocolate bars and
strawberry treats.

Five menorahs[16] with 15 candles burning bright,
Were a very pretty sight.

There was laughing and conversation,
At this holiday celebration.

I grinned when I saw Naomi's son,
Fourteen month old Liam Benjamin.

His eyes were a shining blue,
Like mine and Grandma Peggy's too.

I stood for awhile behind Kimberly's chair,
I was delighted to be there.

Liam was playing on the floor,
I looked at him and grinned some more,

Then I glanced around and I did see,
That Laura, once again, was looking back at me.

She then told Mom that I had come,
To join the others and have some fun.

I was thrilled with my nephew, a cute little boy,
Whom I adore and thoroughly do enjoy.

Many Good Wishes

During the time that I was unwell,
All of the attention was really swell,

To the ICU, Brian's mom, Laurel brought me,
A balloon sculpture of a palm tree.

She also sent me cards a-plenty,
So did Aunt Jackie and my cousin, Wendy.

From friends and relatives, I got many a card and letter.
Saying, how they hoped that I would get better.

From many people, lots of presents came,
Stuffed teddy bears, bunnies, and a lion with a fuzzy
mane.

There were cards from people I had not met,
And Dad printed messages from the internet.

There were pictures, dream catchers, and other things,
From children, there were get well letters and drawings.

Someone also gave on loan, a little bitty Jerusalem stone,
Which Mom and Dad still have at home.

During the two and a half years, when I was sick,
I made friends in many a hospital and clinic.

I was amazed at all the oncology staff would do,
To take care of me and other patients, too.

They coped with all the stress,
Brought on by illness and unhappiness.

Visiting

It is always good to see,
Brian with his wife and family.

And Aviva and Michelle with their children and
spouses.
Sometimes I visit my cousins at their apartments and
houses.

My sisters I see when I have the chance,
I visit them and their husbands, Chris and Lance,

Also, Lisa's step kids Eli, Riley and Maddie, too,
And Naomi's son, Liam, my little nephew.

Both of the girls are now technicians,
Lisa takes X-rays ordered by physicians.

Naomi works with veterinarians,
She helps animals that are carnivores and vegetarians.

I hope this story leaves you believing,
When this life we're finally leaving,

The loved ones who have left before,
Will be there opening up the door.

Then on the other side you'll find,
Friends and relatives, loving and kind.

I'm very busy, with many things to do,
But, I find the time to visit too.

With my friends and with my kin,
Every day, I do check in.

I am just a whisper away,
Morning, noon, and night of every day.

Endnotes

1. In 1909, Kewpie characters were introduced in magazines. Soon, Kewpi Dolls were manufactured. They were cute pudgy baby baby dolls that had some hair sticking up on top of their heads.

2. Leos is short for leotards.

3. AML is the abbreviation for acute myelogenous leukemia.

4. HLA stands for "human leukocyte antigen", a large number of genes that are related immune system functions which are essential elements in immune function.

5. Ruach, breath in Hebrew, signifying spirit, the breath of G-d and also, the meaning of life.

6. Me Sheberach is a prayed for healing.

7. Bubbies and zadies is Yiddish for grandmas and grandpas.

8. In the Old City of Jerusalem, the "Western Wall" or "Wailing Wall" is all that remains of the second temple.

9. At the mountaintop fortress of Masada, near the Dead Sea, 1000 Jews fought Romans from AD 72-73. Many killed themselves and only seven Jewish women and children survived.

10. Be'er Sheva is a city in the Negev Desert.

11. Eretz Yisrael is Hebrew for land of Israel.

12. Canyoning is the combination of rappelling and sliding in waterfalls and streams.

13. The quote "Where there is life, there is hope", originally comes from Ciscero, a Roman philosopher who lived from 106 BC to 43 BC.

14. TNT is the Leukemia Lymphoma Society's Team in Training.

15. Latkes are potato pancakes which are fried in oil to make a special Chanukah food.

16. The menorah is a nine branch candelabra which is lit for eight nights with a Shamesh, a lighter candle which lights one more candle each night until the last, when all nine are lit.